W9-AUD-763

WORLD ALMANAC® LIBRARY OF THE MIDDLE AGES

Churches and Religion

IN THE MIDDLE AGES

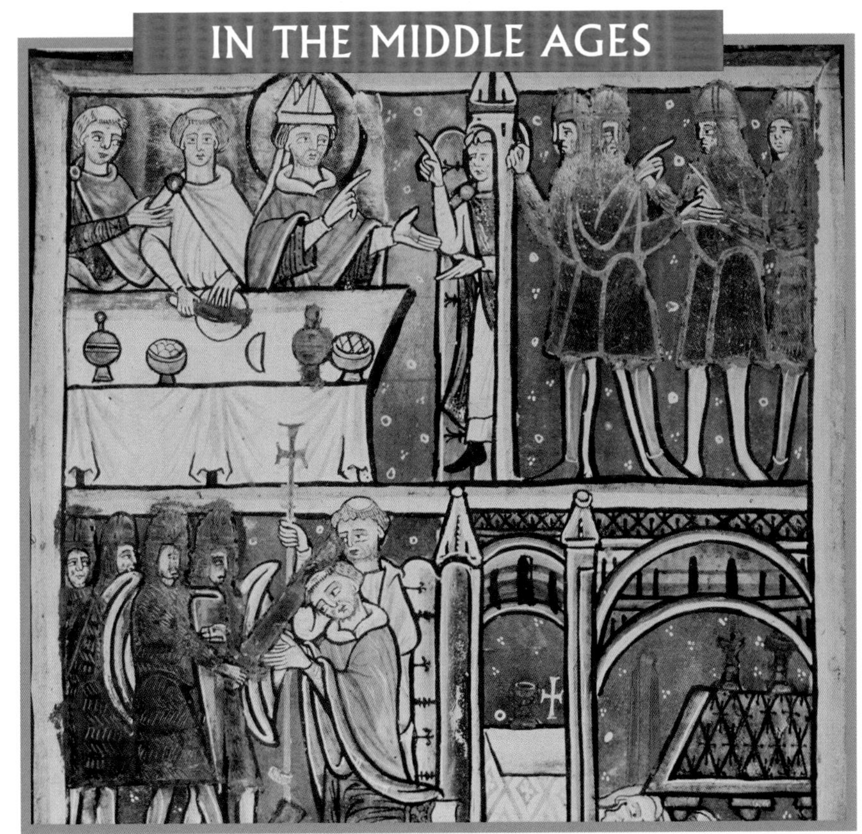

DALE ANDERSON

WORLD ALMANAC® LIBRARY

Please visit our web site at: www.worldalmanaclibrary.com
For a free color catalog describing World Almanac® Library's list of high-quality books and multimedia programs, call 1-800-848-2928 (USA) or 1-800-387-3178 (Canada). World Almanac® Library's fax: (414) 332-3567.

Library of Congress Cataloging-in-Publication Data

Anderson, Dale, 1953-
Churches and religion in the Middle Ages / by Dale Anderson.
p. cm. — (World Almanac Library of the Middle Ages)
Includes bibliographical references and index.
ISBN 0-8368-5892-1 (lib. bdg.)
ISBN 0-8368-5901-4 (softcover)
1. Church history—Middle Ages, 600-1500—Juvenile literature. 2. Religions—History—Juvenile literature. 3. Europe—History—Juvenile literature. I. Title. II. Series.
BR252.A53 2005
270.3—dc22 2005043266

First published in 2006 by
World Almanac® Library
A Member of the WRC Media Family of Companies
330 West Olive Street, Suite 100
Milwaukee, WI 53212 USA

Produced by White-Thomson Publishing Ltd.
Editor: Walter Kossmann
Volume editor: Catherine Burch
Designer: Malcolm Walker
Photo researcher: Amy Sparks
World Almanac® Library editorial direction: Valerie J. Weber
World Almanac® Library editor: Jenette Donovan Guntly
World Almanac® Library art direction: Tammy West
World Almanac® Library graphic design: Kami Koenig
World Almanac® Library production: Jessica Morris and Robert Kraus

Photo credits:
AKG-Images pp. 4 (Archives CDA/St.Genes), cover and 5, 34 (British Library), 7, 36 (Schuetze/ Rodemann), 8 (Pirozzi), 22 (Nimatallah), 25 (Gilles Mermet), 29t (Paul M.R. Maeyaert), 31 (Rabatti–Domingie), 33 (Gerhard Ruf), 40 (Volker Kreidler), 42 (Jean-Louis Nou), 9, 32, 37, 38, 39 (AKG Archive); Art Archive pp. 10 (Viking Ship Museum Oslo/Dagli Orti), 12 (Dagli Orti), 14 (Biblioteca Nazionale Marciana Venice/Dagli Orti), 21 (Musée Condé Chantilly/Dagli Orti), 41, 43 (British Library); Bridgeman Art Library pp. 6, 17 (Bridgeman Archive), 11(Bibliothéque Nationale, Paris), 15 (Private Collection), title page and 19 (British Library, London), 23 (St. Paul's Cathedral Library, London), 29b (Peter Willi), 30 (Ken Welsh).

Cover: A Roman Catholic priest offers ***Mass*** *in this fifteenth-century illuminated manuscript.*
Title page: A manuscript illumination shows the conflict in 1076 between King Henry IV of Germany and Pope Gregory VII about who had the right to name high-ranking Church officials.

Printed in Canada

1 2 3 4 5 6 7 8 9 09 08 07 06 05

Contents

Introduction 4

Chapter 1: Forming the Christian Church 6

Chapter 2: Problems and Reform 10

Chapter 3: Church and State 18

Chapter 4: Crusades, Cathedrals, and Schools 24

Chapter 5: Challenges to the Church 32

Chapter 6: Other Faiths 38

Time Line 44

Glossary 46

Further Information 47

Index 48

Words that appear in the glossary are printed in **boldface** type the first time they occur in the text.

Source References on page 45 give bibliographical information on quoted material. See numbers ([1]) at the bottom of quotations for their source numbers.

The Middle Ages are the period between ancient and early modern times—the years from about A.D. 500 to 1500. In that time, Europe changed dramatically. The Middle Ages began with the collapse of the **Roman Empire** and with "**barbarian**" tribes invading from the north and east. In the early years of the Middle Ages, western European farmers struggled to survive. This period ended with European merchants eagerly seeking new international markets, European travelers searching for lands and continents unknown to them to explore, European artists creating revolutionary new styles, and European thinkers developing powerful new ideas in religion, government, and philosophy.

What Were the "Middle Ages" Like?

Some people view the period as the "Dark Ages," an era marked by ignorance and brutality. It is true that **medieval** people faced difficult lives marred by hard work, deadly diseases, and dreadful wars, but their lives included more than that.

A HISTORIAN'S VIEW

*"A hundred years ago the medieval centuries . . . were widely regarded as 'The Dark Ages.' . . . It was an age whose art was barbaric or '**Gothic**'—a millennium of darkness—a thousand years without a bath. Today . . . scholarship [has] demonstrated clearly that the medieval period was an epoch of immense vitality and profound creativity."*
C. Warren Hollister [1]

The Middle Ages were also a time of growing population, developing technology, increasing trade, and fresh ideas. New villages and towns were built; new fields were cleared; and, with the help of new tools like the wheeled iron plow, farms produced more food. **Caravans** brought silks and spices from faraway lands in Asia. New sports and games, such as soccer, golf, chess, and playing cards, became popular. Musicians, singers, acrobats, and dancers entertained crowds at fairs and festivals. Traveling troupes performed plays that mixed humor with moral messages for anyone who would stop and listen.

Religion, education, and government all changed. Christianity spread throughout Europe and became more powerful. Another major faith—Islam—was born and carried into Europe from the Middle East. New schools and universities trained young men as scholars or

◀ Cathedrals like this one at Chartres, France, stand as impressive monuments of the Middle Ages.

◀ This page from an illustrated book shows Roman Catholic priests celebrating **Mass**, one of the most sacred rituals of the Roman Catholic Church.

or careers in the Church, medicine, and the law. Medieval rulers, judges, and ordinary citizens created **parliaments**, jury trials, and the common law. These changes in the fabric of society still shape our world today.

Historians divide the entire period into two parts. In the early Middle Ages, from about A.D. 500 to 1000, Europe adjusted to the changes caused by the fall of the Roman Empire and the formation of new kingdoms by **Germanic** peoples. In these years, the Christian Church took form and Europeans withstood new invasions. In the late Middle Ages, from about 1000 to 1500, medieval life and culture matured. This period saw population growth and economic expansion, the rise of towns and universities, the building of great cathedrals and mosques, and the launching of the **Crusades**.

Religion in the Middle Ages

Most Europeans in the Middle Ages were Roman Catholics, but some belonged to the Eastern Orthodox Church, to Judaism, or to Islam. Whatever the faith, religion stood at the center of society.

Religion shaped people's lives. People worked every day except for the days they took off once a week to worship and for yearly holidays—"holy days"—set aside for religious celebrations. When people had problems, felt ill, or wished to marry, they turned to their priest, rabbi, or mullah for help.

Religion and government were also closely connected. Islamic, Eastern Orthodox, and Roman Catholic rulers all issued laws in the name of their God.

Finally, religion linked people from different areas. Roman Catholicism united people across much of Europe. People did not see themselves as Europeans but as part of "Christendom"—an area defined by a shared faith. Jews, Muslims, and Eastern Orthodox Christians also felt they belonged to a community of believers—no matter where they lived.

CHAPTER 1

Forming the Christian Church

In the Middle Ages, the Roman Catholic Church dominated European culture and society. Grand cathedrals towered above cities, and Church officials controlled great wealth and power. Priests brought the teachings of the Church to nearly every small village. Yet, the Church began as just a small band of believers in an obscure corner of the Roman Empire, the area of today's Israel and the West Bank.

The Beginnings of Christianity

Christianity is based on the teachings of Jesus, a Jew who lived in the first century A.D. He taught that people should love one another and forgive their enemies. Those who believed in God would be given eternal happiness in heaven after they died. About A.D. 30, Jesus was arrested and accused of treason. The Roman governor of the area had him executed by crucifying him, or nailing him to a cross.

Jesus' followers believed that he was God in human form and that he had saved them by dying on the cross. They believed that Jesus' sacrifice won forgiveness of their sins and eternal life after death.

Why Is It Called "Christianity"?

Jesus' followers believed he was the Messiah. According to Jewish belief, God would send the Messiah to restore the Jewish kingdom and bring about a new age of peace and prosperity. Thus Jesus was called *Christos*, or *Christ*–Greek for "Messiah." Christians, then, are believers in Christ.

Belief in Jesus Spreads

After Jesus' death, his followers carried on his teaching. Early on, a **convert** named Paul began preaching the faith not just to Jews but also to non-Jews. Gradually the faith spread throughout the Roman Empire.

As the religion grew, some Roman officials saw Christians as a problem. Roman law required people to support the official religion. That religion included belief in many gods, one of whom was the Roman emperor. Christians refused to worship these gods, and as a result, some Roman officials **persecuted** them. They arrested believers and even killed some. Despite these attacks, the faith continued to spread.

◀ This wall painting from the mid-third century shows a shepherd with his sheep. Early Christians believed that Jesus cared for all believers just as a shepherd cares for his sheep.

▲ This church, built in the sixth century in Ravenna, Italy, differs from typical medieval Christian churches. Instead of being built in the shape of a cross, as were most churches of that time, this church has eight sides.

)efining the Faith

n the fourth century A.D., Christianity changed ramatically. When the general Constantine ecame the Roman emperor, he ended all ersecution of Christians and declared them ree to worship. The emperor also gave money o build churches and said church officials did ıot have to pay taxes. In A.D. 380, the Emperor 'heodosius went further. He made Christianity he official religion of the Roman Empire.

As Christianity grew, leaders began to build the nstitution that eventually became the Roman 'atholic Church. One step was to decide which vritings would be considered sacred, and these ame to form the Christian Bible. Four books—alled the Gospels—told the story of Jesus and included words he had spoken. Most of these books were written in the first few decades after Jesus' death.

Another important step was to define the core set of ideas that would be official Christian beliefs. Christians living in different areas sometimes had different beliefs. One key difference concerned the nature of Jesus. Most Christians believed that Christ was God in human form. A Christian leader named Arius disagreed. He preached that Jesus was not of the same nature as God, and many Christians adopted this view. This disagreement deeply divided early Christians. In A.D. 325, Constantine ordered a council of Christian leaders to meet in Nicaea, an ancient city in what is now Turkey. This council decided that Arius's teachings were **heresy**.

Organizing the Church

The early Church leaders began to set up an organization. At first, there were no official priests. Elders, who were respected members of each group of worshipers, oversaw services. Eventually, Christians developed two kinds of **clergy**: secular clergy and regular clergy. Priests belonged to the secular clergy. They worked in the world, holding services at local churches and meeting the spiritual needs of ordinary people. Regular clergy were monks who spent their days in work and prayer in communities called **monasteries**.

The position of an elder developed into the office of a bishop. Bishops played key roles in building the Church. They promoted the spread of Christianity in the areas where they worked. They also joined together to strengthen the growing Church. Bishops attended the council at Nicaea and other councils. Some wrote important books explaining what it meant to be a Christian. Three of these writers—Augustine, Jerome, and Ambrose—influenced the Church throughout the Middle Ages. They and other early figures came to be called "Church Fathers."

A few bishops were thought to have the highest status. They included the bishop of Constantinople, the capital of the Roman Empire, and the bishop of Rome. The high place of Rome's bishop stemmed from tradition. Jesus had told his **apostle** Peter that Peter would be the "rock" on which the Church would be built. Since Peter was the first bishop of Rome, later bishops there said they inherited this special authority. Eventually, the bishop of Rome came to be called the pope.

Expansion and Division

While the majority of people in the Roman Empire were Christians, most people living outside it were not. Some were still **pagans**. Many

◀ One task monks performed in their monasteries was to copy books. Some books had pages, like this one from Ireland in the eighth century, decorated with elaborate and colorful illustrations.

thers had adopted Arius's, or Arian, beliefs, not ıose approved at the Council of Nicaea. Through-ut the next few hundred years, Christian leaders evoted much attention to converting the pagans nd Arians. By the late tenth century, though, ıost of Europe—from Ireland to Italy and om Spain to Serbia—was Christian.

While Christianity was spreading, divisions rew between Christians in western Europe and ıose in eastern Europe. One sore point was the ssue of authority. The pope, Leo IX, claimed to e the highest authority in the Church. However, ıe senior bishop in Constantinople—the atriarch, Michael Cerularius—said his authority vas equal. There were differences in beliefs and ractices as well.

These disputes led to a break between the wo areas in 1054. That year, representatives f the pope, Leo IX, declared that the patriarch Iichael Cerularius and all who followed him vere **excommunicated**. The patriarch, in turn, xcommunicated the pope. From that point, ıe Christian Church in the west became known s the Roman Catholic Church. The Church ı the east became known as the Eastern rthodox Church.

Adapting the Church to the People

To gain support among pagans, the Church transformed pagan practices. For instance, the Church turned pagan religious festivals into Christian holidays. The people of Britain and Ireland believed that spirits of the dead walked the Earth on November 1. They followed various rituals to protect themselves from those spirits, including wearing masks and disguises. Hoping to suppress this belief, Pope Gregory IV made November 1 All Saints' Day, a religious holiday. The switch worked—but only partly. Christian converts in the British Isles did honor the **saints** but also kept the older tradition alive. They simply shifted it to the day before, which is now celebrated as Halloween.

▶ This painting shows Augustine blessing the person who paid for the painting while an angel watches. This work from the early fifteenth century shows how respected Augustine remained nearly one thousand years after his death.

CHAPTER 2

Problems and Reform

By the year 1000, the Christian Church was a mature institution. It was also rebounding from attacks by Muslims, Magyars, and Vikings that had damaged or destroyed some churches and monasteries. The next two hundred years saw a new surge of religious feeling among Church leaders and ordinary people. This new feeling brought important changes to the Church.

The Church in 1000

The eighth, ninth, and tenth centuries had brought three waves of invasion to Europe. Muslims, who are followers of Islam, had swept up from North Africa to capture Sicily, southern Italy, and much of Spain. A group called the Magyars had moved into central Europe, attacking towns and villages. They finally settled in what is now Hungary, and they converted to Catholicism. Vikings had stormed down from the north to raid towns and cities. These raiders also plundered monasteries and churches, taking valuable objects and sometimes burning what they left. Like the Germanic peoples before them, the Vikings had settled down by the tenth century and set up new kingdoms. They also joined the Christian Church.

Still, the raids had hurt the Church. Some monasteries had been destroyed, and others had lost members. Partly as a result of the raids, monasteries passed into the control of local nobles, and this weakened them. Some nobles kept the rent money monasteries were supposed to receive for their church lands. Most of the nobles had little interest in forcing the monks to live according to monastic rule. The monasteries continued to exist, but they were no longer centers of prayer and worship. A council of French bishops complained that monks were "forgetful of their profession [and] occupied in worldly business."

GRIEF ABOUT VIKING ATTACKS

"Behold the Church of St. Cuthbert spattered with the blood of the priests of God, despoiled of all its ornaments; a place more venerable than all in Britain is given as a prey to pagan peoples. . . . What should be expected for other places, when the divine judgment has not spared this holy place?"
Alcuin of York, letter [2]

▶ This preserved Viking longship is similar to those used by early Vikings to cross the North Sea to raid monasteries in other parts of Europe.

▲ This painting shows pilgrims near the Church of the Holy Sepulcher in Jerusalem. The church is thought to be built on the site where Jesus' tomb had been.

The Rise of Religious Feeling

The raids and violence produced fears that the Second Coming of Christ was near. That event was supposed to lead to the end of the world and the Day of Judgment. On that day, Jesus would return to Earth and decide the fate of every human. Believers whose sins were forgiven would be saved and allowed to live forever in heaven. Those found too sinful would be condemned to live forever in hell. Fear of this coming event grew throughout the tenth century. Many people were certain that the ending of the first millennium after Christ would see the end of the world. When it did not, there was widespread relief.

Thinking about the Second Coming led to a rise in religious fervor across Europe. These

▲ Santiago de Compostela, Spain, supposedly the burial place of Saint James's bones, is still the destination of pilgrimages by devout Christians.

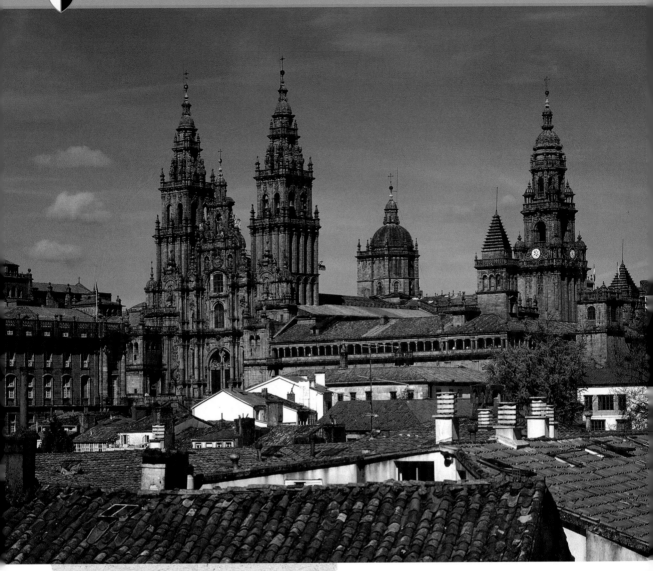

Pilgrimage Sites

Rome and Jerusalem drew pilgrims throughout the Middle Ages. Other sites saw their popularity rise and fall with time. Canterbury, England, held the bones of Thomas Becket, an archbishop who had been murdered and was then made a saint. When word spread that visiting his tomb cured sickness, pilgrims began flocking there, but after just a few years, the site lost its popularity. Santiago de Compostela in Spain remained popular throughout the Middle Ages. Even today, some people take a walking stick and shell, symbols of that pilgrimage, and follow the old route to the cathedral in that city.

deeper feelings of devotion to God continued even after the Second Coming did not happen.

One sign of this growing religious feeling was a rise in the number of people going on **pilgrimages**. The main destinations of these pilgrims were the sites Christians saw as holy. The chief goal was the **Holy Land** and especially Jerusalem, where Jesus had spent his last days. Rome was another important destination for pilgrims, as it held the tombs of Peter and Paul.

PLEDGE FOR PEACE

"No Christian shall kill another Christian, for whoever kills a Christian undoubtedly sheds the blood of Christ."
Council of Narbonne, 1054 [3]

Another popular city was Santiago de Compostela in the northwest corner of Spain. Santiago is Spanish for Saint James, one of Jesus' apostles. In 813, a tomb was discovered near the Spanish city. When miracles began to occur, the local bishop decided that the tomb held the bones of Saint James. Soon people began taking the difficult trek over hard mountain roads to reach this now holy city.

Another sign of renewed religious feeling was the growing popularity of **relics**. Many churches and monasteries claimed to have the bones of a saint or objects from Jesus' life, such as a piece of the cross. The cathedral at Chartres, in northern France, was supposed to hold a piece of the clothing Mary wore when Jesus was born. Pilgrims traveled far to make offerings to these relics. That money went into the treasury of the church or monastery holding the relic.

Seeking a Purer Life and Peace

Some Christians showed their religious feeling by separating themselves from society and living as hermits. They aimed to live a simple, more spiritual life, as the apostles had lived. Some of these people denied themselves all physical comforts and lived completely alone. Others gave up comfort but did not wish to be alone. They settled down with a group of friends, and all devoted themselves to prayer together.

Some people chose to become **anchorites**. These were people who agreed to have themselves sealed in small rooms with only a small window. Once inside, they devoted themselves to prayer and depended on the community to provide food and clothing. A large percentage of these anchorites were women. Some chose this course to avoid marriages that had been arranged for them against their wishes.

The upsurge in religious feeling led to a peace movement. Since Christ's message had been peace, some Christians worked to reduce war and its ill effects. A Church council in France urged that innocent people and clergy be spared harm when two armies fought. Another council went further, declaring that people who fought wars should be excommunicated. As the movement gained support, people came together to pledge that they would not fight.

A related idea was called the Truce of God. People urged that armies refrain from fighting on Sundays and holy days. Later in the eleventh century, the truce period stretched from Wednesday to Monday. Many rulers agreed to the truce—though they often ignored it when

The Role of Saints

Early in the Church's history, some people were recognized as especially holy figures who should be honored, and they came to be called saints. They included Jesus' twelve faithful apostles, Paul, and those **martyred** during the Roman persecutions. In the tenth century, the Church named certain requirements for a person to achieve sainthood. They included leading a moral life and having two miracles credited to him or her.

Saints are honored on a particular date, or feast day. Some saints are considered the patron saints of particular groups. Saint Agnes is the patron of girls, Saint Nicholas of sailors, and Saint Patrick of Ireland. In the Middle Ages, cities and countries staged major festivals on the feast days of their patron saints.

Catholics believe that saints can intervene with God to help them. People also pray to their favorite saint for guidance, or help, when they face a problem.

▲ This illustration from the thirteenth century shows hermits dressed in plain clothing. These religious men gave up most comforts and tried to live simple, pure lives.

convenient. Even though it was not always followed, the peace movement showed a growing desire for more order and stability.

Reform in the Church

The renewed religious spirit swept the Church as well. New leaders aimed to reform the Church and its practices. Leading this movement were several popes, starting with Leo IX. Made pope in 1049, he gathered about him talented monks who were dedicated, like him, to ending abuses

Devotion to Mary

Mary—the mother of Jesus—had always been an important figure among Christians as one of the first people to believe in his mission. The Ave Maria (Hail Mary), a prayer to her, first came into use in the sixth century. In the twelfth century, devotion to Mary gained new popularity. Churches, cathedrals, and monasteries were dedicated to her. Artists sculpted and painted images of her. She was given new titles, including "Queen of Heaven." Preachers said that she would intervene on behalf of people with God. That might explain why she was so popular. Mary remains an important figure in the Roman Catholic Church today.

Electing the Pope

The reformers tried to end outside influence on the Church by changing how the pope was chosen. Originally there were no actual rules for choosing the pope. For centuries, powerful Roman families made the choice, although sometimes they were swayed to pick a particular candidate by the Roman mob or powerful rulers. In 1059, Pope Nicholas II decreed that only cardinals—then a group of bishops who headed particular churches near Rome—had the authority to elect the pope. The new rule was not always applied, however. The reformer Gregory VII was made pope, ironically, by a Roman crowd. Eventually, though, the choice was left to the cardinals alone.

Before he became pope, Gregory I worked as an administrator of papal ıances for several earlier popes. He as particularly interested in ending ›rruption in the Church.

ı the Church and increasing the power of the **apacy**. One of those monks became pope ımself in 1073, taking the name Gregory VII.

One reform was to stop priests from marrying. ntil then, many parish priests and some shops had wives. The reformers believed that ıe clergy needed to focus on caring for the ›iritual needs of people. That meant they should ›t marry. Priests and bishops across Europe protested, and the reform took a long time to take hold. By about 1200, though, married priests were rare.

The reformers took aim at another practice. They wanted to end the custom of buying positions in the clergy, called **simony**. Popes Leo IX and Gregory VII campaigned vigorously against this abuse. While they did not manage to eliminate simony, the practice did become less common.

Building the Papacy

The reformers wanted to increase the power of the papacy. Several popes began to organize Church rules into a system called canon law. Learned men studied Church councils and decrees made by earlier popes. They outlined rules on each problem that the Church faced or each Church teaching. Sometimes it was found that past decrees disagreed with each other, but any questions that still remained were settled by the pope making a final decision. Building the system of canon law helped put more power in the pope's hands.

As the papacy grew stronger, it needed more people to work for it. Popes hired lawyers to work on building canon law. They hired clerks to send messages to Church officials in other lands. To help run this larger papacy, the reformers changed the role of the cardinals. In the eighth century, the cardinals had started helping the popes by doing administrative work. Over time, cardinals were placed in charge of the different departments in the Church's government.

By about 1200, the papacy was a very powerful institution. Historians call it "the papal monarchy" because the pope ruled the Roman Catholic Church as a king ruled a nation.

The Local Church

The pope, of course, was distant from the majority of Christians. Since most people lived in the countryside, they also had little contact with the bishops, who often lived in cities. A parish priest usually represented the Christian Church to most people and instructed and preached to these people. In the early Middle Ages, priests were very similar to the people of their parish. Many were married, and many did not have very much education. By the thirteenth century, the situation was very different. By and large, Church reformers had ceased to allow married priests. The Church made sure that priests were better educated. Priests even began to look different to their **parishioners**. In 1215, a Church council ruled that priests had to wear special clothing.

Priests taught the basic beliefs of the Church to the people of the parish. They led church services and conducted Mass. Priests also heard confessions, when parishioners told them what sins they had committed, and in reply, priests told people what **penance** they had to perform to have their sins forgiven. In 1215, the Fourth Lateran Council made confessing a central part of the Roman Catholic faith for all members of the Church. At least once each year, the council said, each parishioner must confess his or her sins to the parish priest and take part in Easter Mass. Any Catholic who failed to do this could be excluded from the Church.

Finally, the priests were present for three important stages in people's lives. They **baptize** children into the Church, they married couples, and they gave the last rites to the dying.

Parishioners were supposed to give one-tenth of their income, called a tithe, to the local churc That money provided the priest's income. Some priests were in charge of more than one parish. Since they could not be at all of them at the sam time, they put some parishes in the hands of another priest called a vicar. Vicars had the righ to only one-third of the parish income. The rest went to the chief priest. As a result, most vicars were poor and led difficult lives.

With their many responsibilities, priests needed help. Other members of the clergy worke beneath them to provide that help. Those who served as deacons did some of the readings fron the Bible during Mass. If someone had enough learning, he could work as a clerk and help the priest with keeping records and writing letters.

▶ The tower of a church in southern England rises above the parish burial ground. Most Catholics worshiped in village churches like this one, not in the great cathedrals found in cities.

CHAPTER 3

Church and State

Popes were the spiritual leaders of the Catholic world. They also controlled some lands in Italy, just as a prince or king would. These two areas of responsibility—the Church and the State—sometimes led to conflicts between popes and rulers. Some popes claimed that, as God's representatives, they had supreme power on Earth—and thus kings and emperors had to obey them. Some popes clashed with rulers in the effort to protect the lands held by the papacy.

Pope and Ruler

Popes and rulers often confronted a central question: Which of them had the greater authority? Examples from the Roman Empire were confusing. Emperor Constantine had called the Council of Nicaea in A.D. 325, suggesting he had greater authority. On the other hand, he did not interfere in the council's decisions and agreed to follow them. In the fifth century, Pope Gelasius I recognized a split between political and religious power. He said, however, that rulers should obey the Church on matters involving religion.

Two popes, Leo III and Stephen II, took steps that seemed to place their authority—which came from God—higher than that of a ruler. In ancient Israel, holy men poured oil on the head of a king when he was crowned. This act symbolized that the king owed his kingship to God. In 754 and 800, this act was performed when crowning Pepin the Short as king of the Franks and Charlemagne as emperor of Rome. In doing so, the popes showed all Christians that Pepin and Charlemagne received the right to rule from them.

Pope Gregory VII carried the claim of higher authority the furthest. He argued that the pope "is to be judged by no one," but that the pope "may depose emperors." In fact, if the pope believed that a ruler was unjust, he could excuse that country's subjects from any need to obey him. These claims of supremacy led directly to a conflict with King Henry IV of Germany.

The Clash Begins

The dispute between the popes and rulers centered on **lay investiture**, which is the right of a ruler to appoint people to high-level positions in the Church without the pope's approval. King Henry IV of Germany wanted to keep that right, and Pope Gregory VII wanted to take it away. Henry wanted to be able to appoint high Church officials because they owed a king certain duties, such as sending him soldiers when he requested. He wanted to place friends in these offices, so he could count on them to supply those soldiers.

SEPARATION OF CHURCH AND STATE

"There are two powers by which this world is chiefly ruled, august emperor: the sacred authority of the [popes] and the royal power. . . . You know that, even though you surpass the human race in dignity, nevertheless you piously bow your head to those who have charge of divine affairs and . . . in the order of religion, you ought to submit yourself to them rather than rule."

Pope Gelasius I, letter to Emperor Anastasius I [4]

▶ These scenes show the end of the investiture conflict between King Henry IV and Pope Gregory VII. In the top panel, Henry sits at his table with soldiers outside. In the bottom, his troops confront the pope, whose death is shown in the lower right.

Iohes saresbiensis cuidã amico suo.

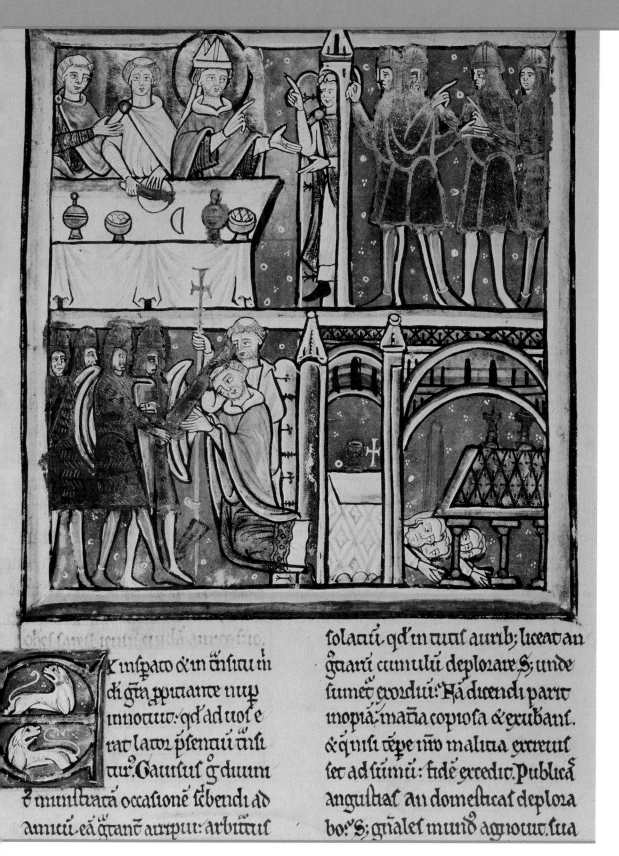

[E]x insperato & in cõsueto in
dei gratia ppitiante nup
innotuit: qd ad uos e
rat lator p̃sentium trãsi
turus. Gauisus g̃ diuini
tus ministratã occasionẽ scribendi ad
amicum eã gratanter arripui: arbitratus

solatium. qd in tutis aurib; liceat an
gustiarũ cumulũ deplorare. S; unde
sumerem exordiũ? Nã dicendi paruit
inopiã: materia copiosa & exubans.
& q̃ nisi tẽpe nro malitia excreuis
set ad sũmũ: fidẽ excedit. Publicas
angustias an domesticas deplora
bo? S; qualis mundus agnouit. sua

The Donation of Constantine

To support their claims of authority, popes pointed to a document called "The Donation of Constantine." The paper was supposedly written by the ancient Roman emperor back in the fourth century. In it, Constantine gave the pope authority over all lands in the western part of the empire. The document was a complete fake created in the eighth century. Nevertheless, popes used it for centuries to justify the idea that rulers had to answer to them. In the fifteenth century, an Italian scholar proved it to be false.

▶ Knights carry out the wishes of King Henry II of England and kill his onetime friend Thomas Becket, the archbishop of Canterbury. The Church moved quickly after Becket's death to name him a saint.

To Pope Gregory, lay investiture contradicted the pope's supreme authority over Church officials and all rulers. Early in 1075, Gregory convinced a Roman Catholic Church council to declare that lay investiture was wrong and that any ruler who carried it out would be punished. Some time later, Henry defied the ruling by naming a new archbishop. The angry pope quickly excommunicated the king and removed Henry from his kingship. Henry called his own Church council. That group, following his orders, excommunicated the pope.

Henry's position was difficult, and German nobles sided with the pope. If the king were weakened, they thought, they would become stronger. Without their support, Henry had to beg forgiveness. He traveled to a castle in northern Italy where Gregory was staying. With wife and child in hand, the king stood in the snow for three days while Gregory figured out what to do. Finally, the pope lifted his order against the king.

Henry then returned to Germany only to find his nobles in revolt. Once Henry had defeated them, he led his army south to Rome. Unable to gather enough support, Gregory had to flee. Henry took the city and put a rival pope in office. That pope cooperated by naming Henry as emperor of the Holy Roman Empire. The Holy Roman Empire was an area made up mostly of modern Germany but also containing parts of Italy. Gregory died in exile a few years later.

Settling the Question

Meanwhile, the issue of lay investiture remained unsettled. In 1122, a new pope, Callistus II, and a new emperor, Henry V, reached an agreement. The pope would fill all Church offices, though the emperor could be present when the selection was made and could step in when there was a dispute. In return, bishops would show their allegiance to the emperor for the lands they held in his name.

However, other rulers were still unwilling to give up the right to fill Church offices. King John of England refused to accept an archbishop named by Pope Innocent III. The pope excommunicated him, and King John was forced to back down. He could not march on Rome, as Henry IV of Germany had done, for it was too far from England. Like Henry, John faced rebellious nobles and had little political support at home.

Even when kings did control appointments to Church offices, their choices could backfire. King Henry II of England named his close friend and adviser Thomas Becket as archbishop of Canterbury. Some years later, Becket was faced with a difficult decision in which he had to choose whether to help the Church or the king. When Becket chose the option better for the Church, an exasperated Henry is said to have called out, "Will no one of my men rid me of this contemptuous, low-born priest?" Four knights promptly rode to Canterbury and murdered Becket. To remove the stain of his role in the murder, Henry had to travel to Canterbury and humble himself by doing public penance.

'opes and Politics

'opes also took part in power politics. In the ighth century, Pepin the Short, king of the Franks, ;ave the papacy control over a wide belt of land in entral Italy, including Rome. This area came to be called the Papal States. From then on, popes were not just the heads of the Roman Catholic Church but also rulers, just like any king. To protect their hold on this land, popes became deeply involved in the politics of Europe. They supported rulers who helped secure their control of the Papal States and opposed those who threatened that control.

Sometimes their strong interest in the Papal States forced them to change sides. In the 1040s and 1050s, large numbers of **Norman** knights came to southern Italy and set up their own kingdom there. At first the popes opposed the Normans, but as the Normans gained success, Pope Nicholas II switched positions. He made a deal with the Norman leader Robert Guiscard. Later, when Guiscard seemed to threaten the Papal States, Pope Gregory VII turned against him. Guiscard won the pope back during the investiture conflict, though. When Henry IV marched toward Rome, Guiscard sent soldiers to defend the pope.

Popes also clashed with rulers about other issues involving control of the Roman Catholic Church. In the late thirteenth century, the kings of England and France were both desperate for money to pay for a war they were fighting against each other. Both decided to force Church officials to pay taxes, which broke tradition. When Pope Boniface VIII ordered the clergy not to pay, King Philip IV of France blocked the flow of Church income from his country to Rome. The pope had to give in.

Popes used their Church powers to help—or hinder—political allies. The Roman Catholic Church did not allow divorce, but sometimes kings wanted to change wives. The pope might agree to annul the marriage of a friendly king but refuse it to rulers who opposed him.

Popes also used their power to help their own families advance. They could give brothers and cousins high-level Church offices or put them in charge of lands that the papacy controlled.

▶ Boniface VIII, pope from 1294 to 1303, issued a strong declaration of the pope's powers. He wrote, "It is altogether necessary for the salvation of every human creature [even rulers] to be subject to" the pope.

▶ This document is an indulgence granted by the bishop of .ondon around 1120. The bishop's seal at the top shows it vas an official document.

Purgatory and Indulgences

Early in the Church's history, a belief arose in a third destination for the dead, in addition to heaven for the saved and hell for those not saved. The third location came to be called purgatory. In purgatory, people who had committed sins but not fully done penance for them could stay until that penance was complete. They, too, could then reach heaven. By praying and doing good works, the living could reduce the time their departed loved ones spent in purgatory. Late in the Middle Ages, the Roman Catholic Church gave people a new way to reduce a soul's time in purgatory. They could buy papers called indulgences. In the early sixteenth century, outrage over that practice led to the Protestant Reformation. That movement broke apart the Roman Catholic Church and eventually led to the rise of Protestantism, Anglicanism, and other religious groups.

The Power and the Glory

ʒy 1200, the Roman Catholic Church was a vealthy institution. Money flowed into the ʼhurch treasury from offerings made at churches. The income from the large estates linked to nonasteries or controlled by bishops also provided wealth.

The funds were used in many different ways. The Church ran hospitals and orphanages and provided aid to the poor. The Church also bought relics to attract the faithful. Bishops ordered paintings, sculptures, and items made of gold, silver, or precious stones to decorate their cathedrals and illustrate God's glory. Some less-religious Church officials used some of the money to support their lives of luxury and comfort.

CHAPTER 4

Crusades, Cathedrals, and Schools

While popes were changing the Church and increasing their own power, the Roman Catholic Church was flexing its muscles. Kings and popes launched crusades—or holy wars—against Muslims. Christians expressed their devotion to God by building magnificent new churches. Brilliant thinkers worked to show how rational thinking could be joined with religious faith.

The Reconquista

In the eighth century, Muslims had conquered much of modern Spain and Portugal. Christian kings, holed up in the north, were determined to win back the land. They launched the movement called the Reconquista, or reconquest.

By A.D.1000, there were five key Christian kingdoms in the **Iberian** peninsula: León, Navarre, Aragon, Castile, and Portugal. The kings of these areas often fought the Muslims. In the eleventh century, León and Castile were joined together and made major gains on Muslim lands. After 1200, Muslim control shrank further, although Muslims kept a toehold in the south. In 1249, the king of Portugal, Alfonso III, reconquered the last part of Portugal from the Muslims. In the late fifteenth century, Isabella of Castile and Ferdinand of Aragon married, thus uniting their major Christian kingdoms. They defeated the last Muslim kingdom in 1492.

The Reconquista brought more people into the Christian Church. Some were Christians who had lived in Muslim lands, and some were Muslims. Christian rulers sometimes allowed these Muslims to continue practicing their faith. Sometimes, though, Muslims were forced to convert or to leave the country. Jews who had lived in Muslim areas were left alone for many decades. Soon after the Reconquista was completed, however, all Jews were ordered to leave Spain unless they converted.

The Reconquista had far-reaching effects. For a long time, scholars in Muslim lands had studied the writings of ancient Greek scientists and philosophers. These works had not been known in western Europe since the end of the Roman Empire. When Christian armies took Muslim cities, these ancient works came into Christian hands. Spanish scholars translated them into Latin and shipped the books to other countries across Europe.

Spain's Hero—El Cid

The Spanish military leader Rodrigo Díaz de Vivar was more commonly known as "El Cid," from the Arabic for "lord." El Cid gained early fame by helping the Christian king of Castile defeat the Muslim king of Zaragoza. Later, however, he angered a key ally of Castile's new king, and the king exiled him. El Cid spent the next ten years fighting for the Muslims, sometimes defeating Christian armies. In 1094, he conquered the city of Valencia for himself. Soon after his death, a long poem emerged. It portrayed El Cid as a warrior of skill, a man of honor, and a hero of the Reconquista. That—and not the more complex reality—is how many Spanish remember him.

▶ In this sculpture from a Spanish church, the Muslim king of Granada gives the keys of the kingdom to Queen Isabella and King Ferdinand. This surrender marked the completion of the Christian reconquest.

Taking Southern Italy for the Faith

The Muslims had also captured Sicily and southern Italy in the ninth century. There, as in Spain, Christians were left alone, though some did convert. Muslim rule brought prosperity, making the region attractive to others. In the 1060s, Normans came to the area determined to conquer it. Their success in 1091 made Christianity the main faith there. The Normans quickly set up monasteries and built churches. Here, as in Spain, Muslim scholarship was translated into Latin, bringing new knowledge.

Still, large numbers of Muslims remained, and the Normans made no effort to force them to convert. Christians and Muslims lived in relative peace for many decades. Over time, however, Christians made life difficult for Muslims, and the followers of Islam left Italy.

Holy War

Between 1095 and 1270, Catholic Europe launched a series of military expeditions called Crusades. Their goal was to take the Holy Land out of Muslim hands. The impetus for the Crusades came from a number of factors. For some years, Muslim armies had been making the journeys of pilgrims to Jerusalem more difficult. Muslim armies had threatened the **Byzantine Empire**, and the emperor asked Urban II for aid. The fighting in Spain and Sicily had created the idea that war against Muslims was just.

Pope Urban II called for the First Crusade in 1095, appealing to Christian knights to march east. The Roman Catholic Church offered to remove all sins of all those who fought. Thousands responded, and a force was on the move by late 1096. The next year, the crusaders reached Asia Minor—what is now Turkey—and defeated a Muslim army at Dorylaeum with overwhelming numbers. In 1098 they won the battle of Antioch and captured several cities in present-day Syria and Israel, including Aleppo and Edessa. Finally, in 1099, they took Jerusalem and killed huge numbers of people, including women and children, in a bloody massacre.

THE MASSACRE IN JERUSALEM

"After [entering Jerusalem] our men rushed round the whole city, seizing gold and silver, horses and mules, and houses full of all sorts of goods, and they all came rejoicing and weeping from excess of gladness to worship at the Sepulcher of our Savior Jesus. . . . Next morning they . . . attacked the [Muslims], both men and women, cutting off their heads with drawn swords. . . . No one has ever seen or heard of such a slaughter . . . and no one save God alone knows how many there were."

Anonymous, *Gesta Francorum*, c. 1100 [5]

The crusaders divided the conquered area into sections ruled by nobles who had joined the fight These were called the Crusader States. Within a few years, the crusaders extended their control in the area by taking some coastal cities.

Later Crusades

In the next few decades, Muslim armies retook Edessa and some of the other areas they had lost to the Christians. In the 1140s, Christians launched the Second Crusade. This failed when King Louis VII of France was unable to capture Damascus (now the capital of Syria). A powerful Muslim leader, Saladin, arose in Egypt and began retaking parts of the Holy Land. In 1187, his forces defeated a Christian army at Hattin, which enabled the Muslims to recapture Jerusalem.

As a result, the Third Crusade began in 1189, led by the kings of England, France, and Germany. The German king accidentally drowned on the way, the other two kings quarreled, and that effort failed to retake the holy city.

In 1204, the army of the Fourth Crusade reached Constantinople, capital of the Byzantine Empire, on the way to the Holy Land. The Crusade's leaders fell into a fierce argument with Byzantine leaders, and as a result, the crusaders attacked the city. They captured it, looted many

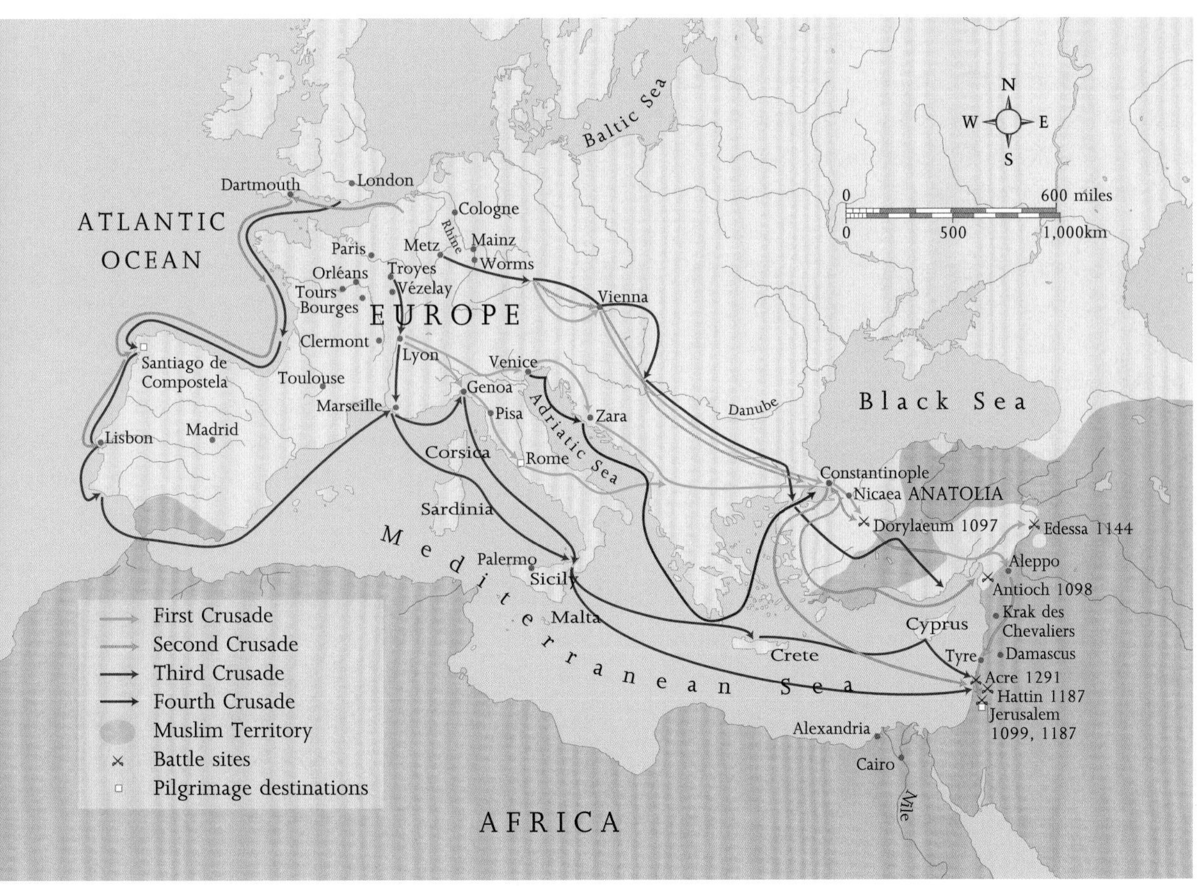

▲ In the First Crusade, crusader victories at Dorylaeum and Antioch, both in present-day Turkey, led to the capture of Jerusalem. Muslims retook Jerusalem in 1187 after defeating the crusaders at the Battle of Hattin. One hundred years later, they captured the last crusader stronghold, Acre, in 1291.

of its treasures, and removed the emperor from power. The Byzantines retook the city in 1261. In the thirteenth century, the crusading spirit dimmed. Three later crusades were also mounted, but they all failed. The Muslims overran the last Crusader stronghold in 1291.

Results of the Crusades

It is often said that the Crusades opened trade between Christian and Muslim lands. In truth, trade was already lively before the Crusades. Sometimes the Crusades are said to have brought Muslim learning into Christian lands. In fact, the conquests of Spain and Sicily played a far greater role in that. The movement certainly did not

The Children's Crusade

One of the strangest episodes of the Crusades was the so-called Children's Crusade. By the early thirteenth century, the crusading movement had lost its zeal. Some people thought that the Christian world should rely on the innocent and mild—children—to succeed where men at arms had failed. Thousands of young boys and girls marched from France and Germany to the Mediterranean. They expected God to part the waters of the sea so they could cross safely to Jerusalem. Many children died on the journey. Many more were captured and sold into slavery. The rest returned, disheartened.

unite Europe's rulers; they bickered and fought one another during and after the Crusades.

The Crusades did have two effects, however, and both were negative. The attack on Constantinople hurt the Byzantine Empire. Although the empire lasted two more centuries, it was smaller and weaker. Also, the wars in the Holy Land deepened the mistrust and bitter feelings between Christians and Muslims.

Building for God

Religious zeal led to the Crusades. It also led to the building of the magnificent cathedrals that stand as a symbol of medieval culture.

A cathedral is a bishop's church. For centuries, cathedrals had been built in a relatively simple style. After A.D. 1000, a new style appeared. It was called Romanesque because it used some of the building techniques that had been used in ancient Rome. The style produced large churches with massive walls and smallish windows. The buildings were larger and more impressive than those built in earlier centuries. Their somewhat dark interiors produced a feeling of religious mystery.

Builders wanted to bring more light into churches. The Gothic style, developed in the mid-twelfth century, achieved that goal. Builders used new techniques to build higher and higher ceilings—many more than 100 feet (about 30 meters). Because these ceilings were made of lighter materials, they could make lighter, thinner walls. They studded the soaring walls with dazzling glass windows. Some of these windows were round and decorated like blooming flowers. Others were made to show pictures that illustrated stories from the Bible or the lives of saints.

The Gothic style began around Paris in the mid-twelfth century and spread quickly. In France alone, dozens of cathedrals were built in the next decades. Huge amounts of stone were needed for this building campaign. From 1050 to about 1350, the French used more stone to build cathedrals than was used in the entire history of ancient Egypt. Other nations adopted the style as well, with local builders using special touches that showed local tastes.

A Community Effort

Each cathedral took many years to build, and each expressed a town's pride. Many skilled craftspeople played a part. Working carefully, stone masons cut and fit the stones. Carpenters built scaffolds the masons had to stand on so they could stack the stones higher and higher into the air. Working away from the building site, glassmakers created the stained-glass windows. Sculptors decorated columns with statues of Jesus, the apostles, and other figures from the Bible. Many people contributed in different ways. Nobles gave money to fund windows that paid tribute to favorite saints. Cloth workers, tanners, and other workers also raised money to pay for windows, which sometimes showed them at their work.

Intellectual Growth

While cathedrals were being built, Church thinkers began exploring great questions of faith. Some of their thinking was just as dazzling as the new Gothic churches.

The Church had been committed to learning from the start. Church officials needed to write clearly to explain Church teachings. Monks in monasteries copied important writings about the religion to save them for later generations to read.

In the twelfth and thirteenth centuries, there was a new burst of intellectual activity. One reason was the new chance to read ancient Greek works that were now available in western Europe after the conquest of Muslim lands in Spain and southern Italy. Another cause was the rise of schools that were part of some of the great cathedrals. These schools eventually gave rise to the first universities. In these universities, scholars gathered to study law, medicine, and—most importantly—**theology**.

▲ The interior of Chartres Cathedral (*above*) shows the soaring ceilings and feeling of lightness that marked the Gothic style. The photograph on the right reveals some of the stained-glass windows that filled the high walls of Chartres and other Gothic cathedrals.

THE PURPOSE OF STAINED GLASS

"[We will fill the church] with the most radiant windows . . . [to] illumine people's minds so that they may travel through light to an apprehension of God's light."

Abbot Suger, *De Consecratione Ecclesiae*, 1140s [6]

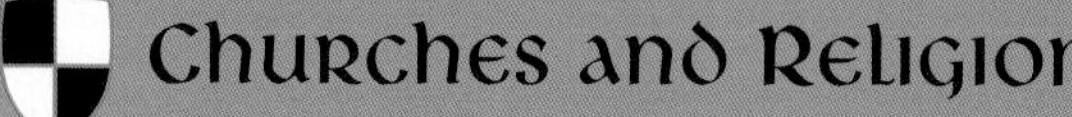

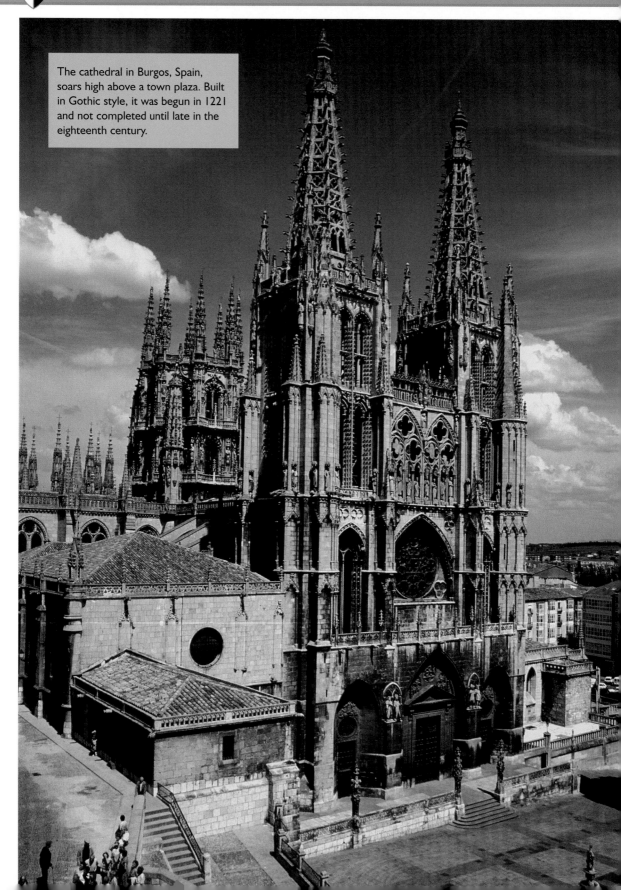

The cathedral in Burgos, Spain, soars high above a town plaza. Built in Gothic style, it was begun in 1221 and not completed until late in the eighteenth century.

◀ Thomas Aquinas, seated, instructs a group of students.

Those who studied theology developed a way of thinking called **scholasticism**. They tried to use logic to find a rational basis for faith. This drive was, in effect, another kind of crusade. The crusaders had used weapons to conquer Muslim lands. The scholastics wanted to use reason to show that Christianity was more logical than Islam.

The leading scholastic was Thomas Aquinas. The scholastics collected their writings into books of many volumes called summa. Aquinas's summa was on the subject of theology. He argued that the mind can apply reason to the knowledge gained from the senses and prove the existence of God.

Thomas Aquinas
(c. 1224–1274)

Born in Italy, Thomas Aquinas became the foremost philosopher of the Middle Ages. Aquinas was placed by his family in a monastery while still young. After several years, he was sent to the University of Naples. There he read some of the works of ancient Greek philosophy that were just reaching Christian Europe from former Muslim lands. Excited by what he read, Aquinas continued his studies. By 1256, he began to teach at the University of Paris. For the rest of his life, he lived in the midst of a swirling current of ideas that tried to see how both faith and reason could lead to the truth. After his death, the Catholic Church ruled that some of his ideas were wrong. Later, though, his writings were adopted as Church **doctrine**, and he was made a saint.

CHAPTER 5

Challenges to the Church

Many challenges to the Church plagued the Roman Catholic religion in the late Middle Ages. Some people called for a simpler way of life and openly criticized the Church. The writings of mystics who claimed that they had had religious experiences and direct contact with God seemed to make the Church unnecessary. Meanwhile, amid charges of corruption and unfair politics, the papacy fell into chaos.

Back to Basics

The growing power and wealth of the Roman Catholic Church seemed to go against the teachings of Jesus to some Christians. They rejected Church practices and authority in an effort to lead a more humble life that they thought showed greater devotion to God.

In the 1170s, Peter Waldo, a wealthy merchant in Lyons, France, heard the story of a saint who had adopted poverty. Inspired, he decided to

▼ This wall painting from a church in Florence shows Pope Innocent III giving his blessing to Francis of Assisi and his rule for Franciscan friars.

ORDERED POVERTY

"[The Poor Clares] are not to receive or hold onto any possessions or property . . . except as much land as necessity requires for the integrity and the proper seclusion of the monastery; and this land is not to be cultivated except as a garden for the needs of the sisters."
Clare of Assisi, *Rule*, 1212 [7]

ollow the example. He began preaching in public o convince others to adopt this simpler life. Soon Valdo gathered a following, called Waldensians.

The same impulse moved Francis of Assisi, a leeply religious man, in the early thirteenth entury. Francis, the son of an Italian merchant, egan giving his money and clothing to the poor nd sick. Eventually, he decided to found a new rder within the Catholic Church. He called his ollowers *friars*, from the Latin for "brothers." 'rancis's rules for the order were strict. Brothers ad to preach and work for the poor every day. 'hey wore simple brown robes and owned as ew possessions as possible. They could not ven touch money and had to beg each day for helter and food. Francis wanted them to carry he message of God to the people and inspire thers to belief through their example of poverty.

The Franciscan order grew rapidly. Formed n 1210, more than fourteen hundred houses for he friars had been founded by 1300. Francis's xample inspired a follower named Clare to found similar order for women. The Poor Clares, as hey were called, also spread quickly. There was difference, though. Franciscans were active in he world, preaching in the cities. The Church did ot want single women moving about in public, nd they made the Poor Clares live in seclusion.

Some people adopted lives of poverty without vithdrawing from the world. Women called 3eguines dedicated themselves to helping the

▲ Clare of Assisi, shown here, was named a saint by the Church just two years after her death in 1253.

poor and sick. Some men joined this movement as well; they were called *Beghards*.

Fighting Heretics

The Church eyed some of these movements warily. Groups like the Franciscans who recognized obedience to the Church were welcome. The Waldensians, though, preached against Church officials for being more interested in wealth than matters of the spirit. Not surprisingly, their beliefs were labeled as heresy. The Church made some efforts to end the movement, but it survived by meeting in secret.

The Church also attacked other movements, especially the Cathars of southern France. This group believed that two gods, one good and one evil, struggled to rule the world. The Cathars said the Church followed the evil god. In 1209, Pope

The Inquisition

To root out heresy, the Catholic Church created what became a famous system of trials called the Inquisition. Over the years, the Inquisition gained a frightening reputation. Trials were held in secret. Witnesses who spoke against accused **heretics** did so without the accused person's knowledge. Since defending a heretic was itself a crime, no lawyers were willing to help the accused. Torture was permitted as a way of winning a confession. The penalty for guilt was death. In the Middle Ages, however, Inquisition trials led to the execution of only about two thousand people. More were victims in later periods. An order of friars—the Dominicans—often carried out the trials. Founded by a Castilian, Domingo de Guzman, this order devoted itself to learning theology. Church leaders believed that the Dominicans' deep study put them in a position to identify heresy. Their skill at exposing heretics produced a popular pun on their names. The Dominicans were sometimes called by the Latin words *Domini canes*, which means "hounds of the lord (or God)."

nnocent III called for a crusade against them and ısed Church funds to finance the army. Soldiers narched into southern France and killed tens of housands of Cathars.

In the mid-fourteenth century, John Wycliffe of :ngland preached that the Church should return o its roots and adopt poverty. He, too, rejected he authority of Church officials. Thinking that ıll believers should have access to the Word of ;od, he urged that the Bible be translated from .atin into common languages, such as English. ıfter his death, Wycliffe's ideas were condemned as heresy. Church officials sought out and punished his followers.

Wycliffe's ideas, however, had reached Bohemia in central Europe. In about 1400, they were adopted by a preacher named John Hus. The Hussite movement grew popular and was seen as increasingly dangerous. Some of Hus's followers wanted to weaken the hold of the Holy Roman Empire on their land. This threat to both the Church and the rule of Emperor Sigismund was too great to be allowed to continue. The Church called Hus to a Church council. There he was seized, convicted of heresy, and burned at the stake. Hus's execution ignited a revolt in Bohemia.

◀ This illustration shows French soldiers driving efeated Cathars out of the city of Carcassonne, in outhern France. This city was one of the strongholds f the Cathar movement.

Church Mystics

Some pious Christians—called mystics—had deep and life-changing religious experiences. Through these experiences, they felt that they achieved union with God. This message of direct contact with God sometimes alarmed Church officials. Meister Eckhart was a popular German preacher. Although he was a Dominican, the Church condemned some of his ideas as heretical. Marguerite Porete of France—another mystic—was tried in Paris and executed by the Inquisition.

A MYSTIC'S NEAR-DEATH EXPERIENCE

"When I was thirty years old and a half, God sent me a bodily sickness, in which I lay three days and three nights; and on the fourth night I took all my rites of Holy Church, and [expected] not to have lived till day.

I . . . set my eyes on the face of the Crucifix. . . . After this my sight began to fail, and it was all dark about me in the chamber, as if it had been night, save in the image of the Cross whereon I beheld a common light. . . . And in this [moment] suddenly all my pain was taken from me, and I was as whole . . . as ever I was before."

Julian of Norwich, *Revelations of Divine Love*, c. 1400 [8]

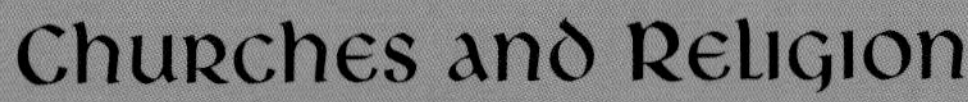

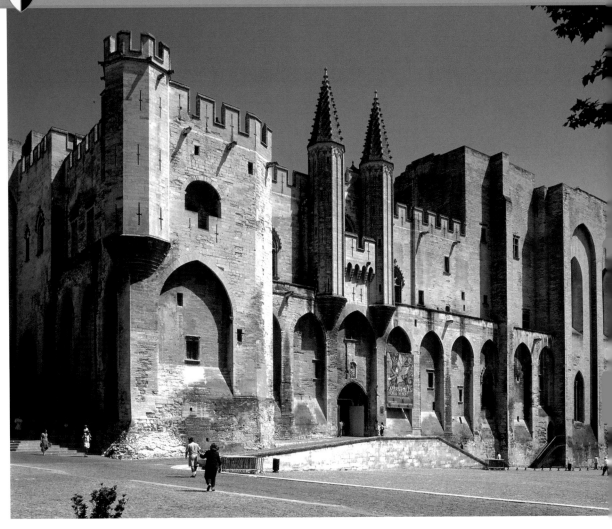

▲ The palace used by the popes at Avignon, shown here, looks more like a fortress than a palace.

Many mystics were left alone, however, and some even enjoyed honored status within the Church. A woman named Julian of Norwich lived as an anchoress at the cathedral at Norwich, England, until her seventies. Hildegard of Bingen, a German nun and a mystic, was highly respected. Heads of monasteries asked her advice. Members of the clergy also sought her views on theology.

Discredit and Schism

While the Roman Catholic Church was challenged by heretics, serious problems beset the papacy. In 1309, Pope Clement V moved himself and the government of the Church to Avignon, a city in France. For nearly seventy years, he and several succeeding popes led the Catholic Church from this city, not Rome. The popes lost some moral authority in these years. One reason was that they tended to favor France in disputes between countries. As a result, they could no longer claim that they treated everyone equally. Another factor was the rich and luxurious life led by Church officials in France.

What followed was even worse. In 1378, Pope Gregory XI returned to Rome but died soon after. After Urban VI was elected, the cardinals turned against him. They moved back to Avignon, declared his election null, and chose a new pope, Clement VII. From 1378 to 1415, two rival popes ıeaded the Roman Catholic Church, one from Rome and one from Avignon. Political rivalries in Europe shaped which pope different rulers chose o follow. France and its allies favored Clement. England, Germany, and other countries sided vith Urban. For the next several decades, the hurch was split by the conflicting orders of ival popes. This division is called the Great chism (a *schism* is a break). Starting in 1409 here was even a third pope, based in Pisa, Italy. Ie was Alexander V, and he had been elected y a Church council.

Restoring Order in the Church

'he problem of multiple popes was finally settled n 1415. The Holy Roman Emperor Sigismund nd Pope John XXII—who had succeeded Alexander V in Pisa—called a Church council. Bishops from across Europe met in Constance, Germany. John XXII took part at first but then fled the city, hoping his departure would leave the council without authority—and leave him in power. Emperor Sigismund forced the council to continue working without John XXII. In the end, it agreed to unseat all three popes and elect a new one.

The new pope, Martin V, brought the papacy back to Rome. During his rule, he summoned other councils. They made decisions that Church leaders in all lands agreed to follow. This helped reunite the Church. The papacy had become weakened by all the disputes, however. Councils became very important in leading the Church in the next few decades.

◀ Emperor Sigismund, shown here, was vital to the success of the Council of Constance. He wanted it to not only solve the problem of the popes but move against John Hus. Hus's followers were causing turmoil in Bohemia, part of Sigismund's empire. Sigismund wanted the Church to condemn the Hussites so he could have the backing of its authority to crack down on them.

CHAPTER 6

Other Faiths

atholic Christianity was not the only faith of medieval Europe. In the Byzantine Empire and other lands in eastern Europe, people followed the Eastern Orthodox Church. Muslims ruled some lands on the northern shores of the Mediterranean. Jews lived scattered throughout Europe, where they sometimes faced harsh treatment from Christians.

Differing Churches

During the early days of Christianity, churches in the eastern and western halves of the Roman Empire differed in many ways. Some differences were central to their beliefs. They disagreed on the exact relationship of the three aspects of God—the Father, the Son, and the Holy Spirit. They argued about what kind of bread should be used in the Mass. Even the date for celebrating Easter was a matter of dispute. They also differed over leadership. Bishops in western churches were guided by the pope, the bishop of Rome. Those in the east paid more attention to the patriarch, the title given the bishop of Constantinople.

The split between the two groups of churches became final in 1054. That year, Pope Leo IX and Patriarch Michael Cerularius had angrily excommunicated each other. The Church in the west came to be called the Roman Catholic Church. The eastern Church became the Eastern Orthodox Church.

The Eastern Orthodox Church was closely linked to the Byzantine Empire. Emperors had some influence on the Church and on the naming of Church officials. Emperors, however, were not allowed to make decisions about major beliefs in the Church.

As in the west, the Eastern Orthodox Church tried to convert people who were pagans. Missionaries went to present-day Russia, Ukraine, Bulgaria, and other regions to convert people. As churches developed in these areas, each had its own chief bishop, who went to Church councils. In the Eastern Orthodox Church, these councils had the highest authority. The patriarch commanded the respect of the other bishops, but they did not have to obey him. The patriarch, then, had less power over the Eastern Orthodox Church than the pope had over the Roman Catholic Church.

A focal point of the Eastern Orthodox Church was the impressive cathedral called the Hagia

▲ This fourteenth-century Russian painting of Saint Demetrius shows the influence in Russia of the art of the Byzantine Empire. When the Russians converted to the Eastern Orthodox faith, they adopted Byzantine culture.

A VISITOR'S VIEW OF THE HAGIA SOPHIA

"The Greeks led us to the edifices where they worship their God and we knew not whether we were in heaven or on earth. For on earth there is no such splendor or such beauty, and we are at a loss how to describe it. We only know that God dwells there among men and their service is fairer than the ceremonies of other nations. For we cannot forget that beauty."
Envoys of Prince Vladimir of Kiev, writing back to the prince, A.D. 987 [9]

▲ The Hagia Sophia (*above*) still stands in Istanbul, formerly known as Constantinople, in Turkey. Today it serves as a mosque, but some decorations, such as a mosaic portrait of Jesus, show its origins as a Christian church.

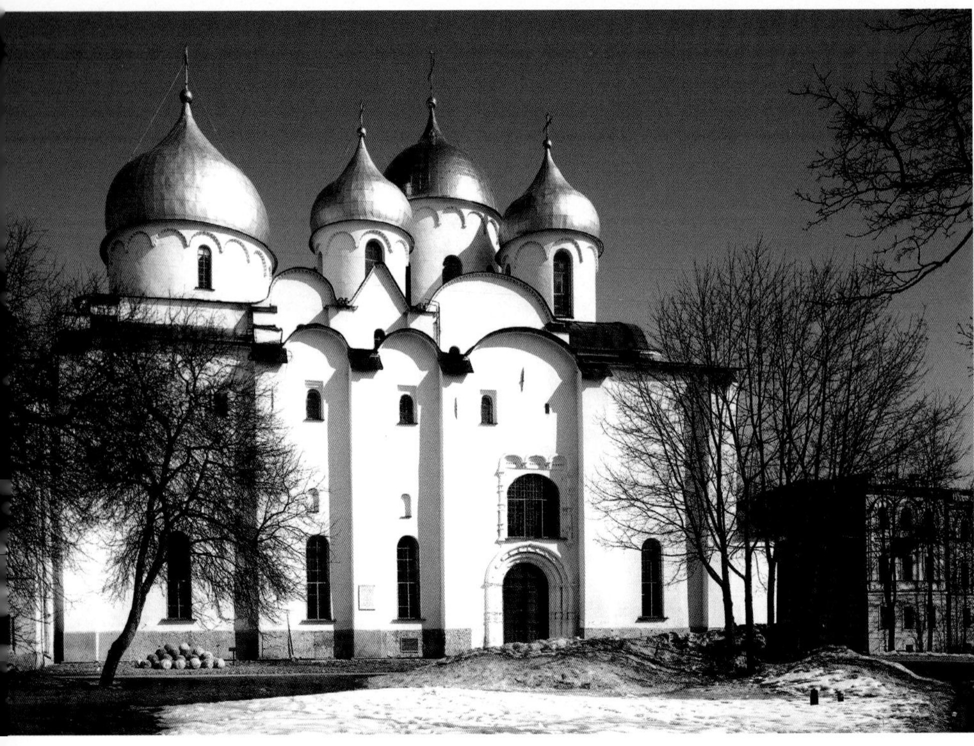

◀ Onion-shaped domes top the towers of many Russian churches, such as this cathedral in the city of Novgorod.

Converting the Slavs

In the ninth century, the monks Cyril and Methodius were dispatched from Constantinople to present-day Bulgaria and nearby lands, where they converted the Slavs. In the process, they invented an alphabet for writing Slavic so they could translate the Gospels into that language. That system—called Cyrillic after one of the monks—is still used in Russia and other Slavic lands today. Russia joined the Eastern Orthodox Church in the tenth century, when Prince Vladimir of Kiev adopted the faith.

Sophia, or the Church of the Holy Wisdom. It was built in Constantinople by Justinian, emperor of the Byzantine Empire in the mid-sixth century. For many centuries, it was the most magnificent church in the entire Christian world.

A New Religion: Islam

Starting in the eighth century, the Byzantine Empire was seriously challenged by a series of conquests made in the name of a new religion, Islam. Followers of Islam believed that the founder of the religion, Muhammad, received revelations from God. Born in about 570, Muhammad proclaimed that there was only one God, Allah, and that people had to submit to God's will. *Muslim*, the term for believers in Islam, means "one who submits."

In the early seventh century, Muhammad's faith spread quickly across the Arabian peninsula. Within a century, Muslim armies had conquered a huge stretch of land from modern Iran to Spain and all along the eastern and southern shores of the Mediterranean. Eventually they also took parts of southern Italy.

Muslim law united the different peoples living in this huge territory. The Arabic language linked them as well. Arabic was the language of the Koran—the Muslim holy book. Muslims believed that the words of Allah could only be understood by reading them in Arabic. Converts learned Arabic, then, to better understand the faith and to take part in prayers.

Muslims—like Christians—believed that their

eligion was the one, true faith and that only elievers would enjoy eternal happiness in aradise. Still, they did not try to win converts in e same way Christians did. Those people who ished to convert could convert; it was a matter f choice. Non-Muslims quickly noticed, however, at Muslims had more privileges than they. That ct led many non-Muslims to adopt the faith.

In Islam, Christians have special status ecause Muhammad recognized Jesus as a orthy prophet. In Muslim-held lands in the Middle Ages, Christians had to pay the same tax all non-Muslims had to pay, but they enjoyed some privileges other non-Muslims did not. They were usually allowed to worship as they wished, though they could not try to convert Muslims. Christians were usually not persecuted, either. Many Christians in Muslim lands decided to convert to Islam. In fact, the majority of the population in Spain became Muslim.

The Five Pillars of Islam

Five practices show a Muslim's devotion to Islam. They are:

- Making a declaration of faith: "There is no God but Allah, and Muhammad is his messenger."
- Praying five times a day, every day
- Donating money to charity, which is used to care for the poor
- Fasting during daylight hours each day of the holy month of Ramadan
- Making a pilgrimage to the holy city of Mecca, in today's Saudi Arabia, at least once, if possible

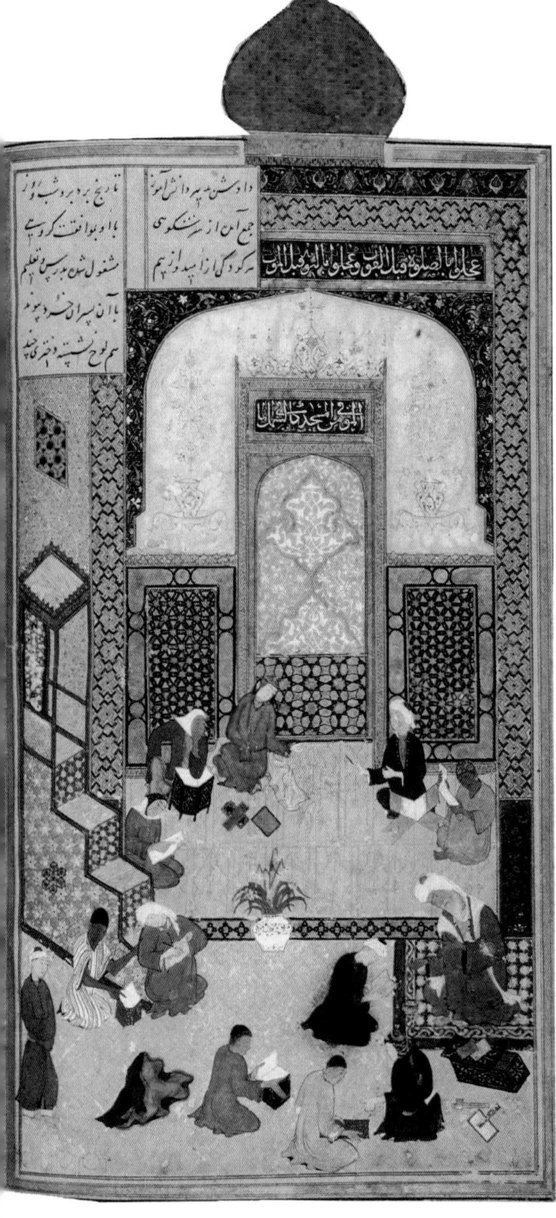

Christian treatment of Muslims followed similar patterns. In some periods, they were tolerated and allowed to practice their religion. For instance, as Christian rulers in Spain and southern Italy took Muslim lands, they often left Muslims alone. Over time, though, Muslims living in Spain and southern Italy suffered harsher treatment. Some converted to Christianity, sometimes because they were forced to do so by rulers, and others left for Muslim lands.

Jews in Muslim and Christian Lands

The Muslims who ruled Spain and southern Italy generally tolerated Jews in their lands as well. Islam sees the prophets of the Old Testament, on which the Jewish religion is largely based, as part of its tradition. Muslim Spain had a thriving

◀ This miniature painting from the late fifteenth century shows Muslims at school. The walls, as in many rooms in Muslim buildings, are decorated with complex patterns.

▲ These columns form part of the interior of the magnificent mosque built by Muslim rulers in Córdoba, Spain, from 785 to 990. After Christians took the city in th thirteenth century, they turned the building into a cathedra

Moses Maimonides
(1135-1204)

The Jewish philosopher Moses Maimonides was born in Muslim Spain. When he was in his teens, the Almohads took power, and his family eventually left. He spent the rest of his life in North Africa and Europe. Trained as a physician, he was also a rabbi, or Jewish religious teacher. In that role, he wrote an important book about Jewish law. Maimonides is most famous, though, for his book *A Guide for the Perplexed*, which he finished in 1191. In it, he tried to reconcile reason and religion. The book was widely read by both Jewish and Christian thinkers.

Jewish community, which enjoyed something of a golden age in the tenth to the early twelfth centuries. Leading Jews served as close advisors to Muslim rulers. Many Jews thrived in the booming economy. Physicians advanced their science, and philosophers thought and wrote about the nature of faith. Jewish poets wrote moving poems that helped keep the Hebrew language alive.

That golden age ended in the early twelfth century, when a more extreme group of Muslims called the Almohads came to power in Spain. Th Almohads forced Jews to convert to Islam or leav he country. Some Jews pretended to convert but ontinued to practice Judaism secretly. Many left, raveling to other Muslim lands or to Christian ingdoms in Spain or elsewhere in Europe.

In most of Christian Europe, Jews lived ifficult lives. They were not always persecuted; ometimes they were grudgingly tolerated, but ney always lived on the edge of society, unable ɔ predict when rulers or common people would ırn against them.

Sometimes they were subjected to vicious ttacks. The first major one came in 1095 during ne First Crusade. On their way to the Holy Land, n army of crusading knights attacked Jews in everal German towns. They massacred many eople, including men, women, and children. hey also robbed, taking all the victims' aluables. This was not the last time that Jews uffered such attacks. The worst violence came ı the middle to late fourteenth century, when the **lack Death** raged across Europe. In some areas, ews were falsely accused of causing the deadly isease by poisoning wells. Mobs in many towns om Germany to Spain killed innocent Jews.

Even where they were allowed to live, Jews ere often treated unfairly. Laws blocked them om entering some professions. Other laws ɔrced them to live only in certain areas in towns. he Catholic Church ruled in 1215 that all Jews ad to wear special badges on their clothing to lentify them. Sometimes rulers forced them to ave the country, which happened in England in 290 and in France in 1306. In both cases, the eason was simply royal greed—the kings seized neir lands and property to enrich themselves.

For many centuries, the lives of Jews in Spain ere somewhat better. When Christian kings took ınd from Muslim rulers, they continued to allow ews to practice their religion. One Christian king, eter IV, let the Jews of Toledo build a new **ynagogue**. Later, though, the position of Jews ecame more difficult. In a sudden eruption of iolence, thousands of Jews were killed in 1391. he cause was another outbreak of the Black eath, for which Jews were once again wrongly

▲ In this illustration from a 1350 manuscript from Barcelona, Spain, a Jewish family celebrates the religious holiday of Passover. During Passover, Jews recall the time thousands of years ago when God freed them from slavery in Egypt. During the Middle Ages, Jews did not live in slavery, as they had in ancient Egypt, but they were often persecuted and sometimes expelled from the lands where they lived.

blamed. In later years, many Spanish Jews were forced to convert to Christianity. Even then, the converts were not trusted as being true Christians. Finally, in 1492, all Jews were expelled from Spain.

Spain also forced Muslims to leave the country or to convert to Christianity. The change seemed to be a great triumph for the Spanish rulers—and for the Roman Catholic Church. In the next century, though, the Catholic hold on Europe would be broken by the Protestant Reformation. That movement saw millions of people move into new churches that were being formed. Nevertheless, in this later period, as during the Middle Ages, religion remained a vital part of European life.

312
Constantine declares Christianity legal in the Roman Empire.

325
Constantine calls Church council at Nicaea.

380
Theodosius I makes Christianity the official religion in the Roman Empire.

476
The end of the reign of the last Roman emperor in western Europe marks the end of the Roman Empire.

537
Hagia Sophia, a Christian church, is completed in Constantinople, now known as Istanbul.

622
Muhammad moves to the city of Medina and recruits followers, marking the beginning of Islam.

711
Muslims enter Iberia and begin the conquest of Spain.

c. 755
The Papal States are created. This is the territory in Italy controlled by the pope.

900s
Fears rise that the Day of Judgment is coming when the millenium ends.

900s-1100s
The Jews in Muslim Spain prosper during a "Golden Age."

965
Muslim forces capture Sicily and some of southern Italy.

1000s
Religious feeling becomes more intense through much of Europe and the number of people going on pilgrimages increases.

1049
Pope Leo IX becomes the first of several reformer popes.

1054
The Roman Catholic Church and Eastern Orthodox Church split.

1070s
Pope Gregory VII and King Henry IV of Germany clash over investiture issue.

1075-1125
The period when churches are built in the Romanesque style in western Europe.

1091
The Normans complete the takeover of Muslim Sicily.

1095
Pope Urban II calls for a crusade; the First Crusade begins the following year.

1099
Crusaders capture Jerusalem, and the success of the First Crusade leads to the creation of the Crusader States in the Holy Land.

1137-1144
The church of Saint-Denis, near Paris, France—the first Gothic church in Europe—is constructed.

1122
An agreement between Pope Callistus II and Emperor Henry V ends the investiture conflict.

1204
Crusaders of the Fourth Crusade take Constantinople.

1209-1229
The Church carries out a crusade against the Cathars in southern France.

1209
Pope Innocent III approves the Franciscan order.

212
housands of French and German children go n the Children's Crusade, which collapses.

216
ope Honorius III approves the Dominican rder, whose members lived in poverty.

256
homas Aquinas begins teaching at the niversity of Paris.

291
luslims capture Acre, the last Crusader city.

309
lement V moves papacy to Avignon, France.

347
he plague, or Black Death, breaks out for the rst time in medieval Europe.

378-1415
he period known as the Great Schism, during vhich time rival popes rule in both Rome nd Avignon.

391
nti-Jewish violence in Spain results in the eath of thousands of Jews.

411
ohn Wycliffe's works are declared full f heresy.

414-1418
ouncil of Constance meets, reforming the hurch. The Council also declares John Hus heretic and executes him.

453
luslim Ottoman Turks capture Constantinople, nding the Byzantine Empire.

492
sabella and Ferdinand capture Granada, the ast Muslim possession in Spain, marking the nd of the Reconquista.

Source References:

1. C. Warren Hollister, *Medieval Europe: A Short History*, Wiley, 1964, p. 1.

2. Alcuin of York. Quoted in J. A. Hoeppner Moran Cruz and R. Gerberding, *see above*, p. 193.

3. Council of Narbonne. Quoted in J. A. Hoeppner Moran Cruz and R. Gerberding, *see above*, p. 267.

4. Gelasius I. Quoted in J. A. Hoeppner Moran Cruz and R. Gerberding, *see above*, p. 278.

5. Gesta Francorum. Quoted in J. A. Hoeppner Moran Cruz and R. Gerberding, *see above*, p. 299.

6. Abbot Suger. Quoted in the web site of the Archdiocese of Detroit, Cathedral of the Most Blessed Sacrament section, "A Cathedral Narrative."

7. Clare of Assisi Rule. Quoted in J. A. Hoeppner Moran Cruz and R. Gerberding, *see above*, p. 434.

8. Julian of Norwich. Quoted from Chapter III of *The Revelations of Divine Love* in the Christian Classics Ethereal Library at the Calvin College web site.

9. Quoted in E. Peters, *Europe and the Middle Ages*, second edition, Prentice Hall, 1989, p. 65.

anchorites/anchoresses People who decide to live a secluded life away from others in a small cell and devote themselves to prayer
apostles The twelve closest followers of Jesus, who traveled with him as he preached and who spread belief in him after his death
baptized Blessed a person with water in a Christian rite that symbolizes the person's acceptance into the Christian Church
barbarian An ancient Greek word used by Romans and later Europeans to describe foreigners. It suggests that foreigners are wild, brutal, and savage.
Black Death Name given to the bubonic plague, a disease that swept across Europe in the mid-fourteenth century and returned several times thereafter. It killed huge numbers of people, perhaps as much as one-third to one-half of Europe's population.
Byzantine Empire The empire that had been the eastern part of the Roman Empire and was based in Constantinople and lasted until 1453.
caravans Travelers who group together to help each other, usually in a hostile region, such as a desert
clergy People recognized by the Church as having the authority to perform religious services
convert A person who has adopted a new religion
Crusades Wars fought between Christians and Muslims, pagans, or heretics
doctrine An official system of religious belief
excommunicated Declared that a member of the Church has done something so wrong that he or she is officially expelled from it; loyal Church members were supposed to avoid contact with that person and no longer owed him or her obedience.
Germanic Related to German-speaking peoples, such as the Goths, Visigoths, and Franks, who moved into western Europe in the later centuries of the Roman Empire and set up several new kingdoms after the fall of the western Roman Empire
Gothic A style of church architecture developed in the mid-twelfth century marked by very tall churches, relatively thin stone walls, narrow column supports, pointed arches, and large amounts of stained glass
heresy A belief that differs from official Church beliefs
heretics People who disagree with or dissent from established religious beliefs
Holy Land The areas of modern Israel and the West Bank believed to be holy by Christians because Jesus Christ lived and taught there
Iberian Refers to the region of southwestern Europe that is now occupied by Spain and Portugal
lay investiture Right of a ruler to appoint people to high Church positions without the approval of the pope
martyred Put to death for one's beliefs or faith
Mass The rite that includes the ritual eating of bread and drinking of wine that is part of Roman Catholic services; the two substances symbolize the body and blood of Jesus, and the ritual recalls the last meal he shared with his apostles.
medieval A word that relates to and describes the Middle Ages
monasteries Communities of clergymen, called monks, who pray, work, and live according to a strict rule
Norman A member of a Viking tribe who settled in northern France
pagans A term used by Christians to refer to the religions of the Romans and Germanic peoples, who worshiped many gods; now means person with no religion
papacy The office of the pope and all the parts of the administration of the Roman Catholic Church that the pope controls
parishioners People who live in a parish (the area attached to a church)
parliament A conference to discuss public affairs, or the organization of political groups to form a government
penance Actions that a person can take to win forgiveness of his or her sins
persecuted Caused to suffer because of one's beliefs
pilgrimages Journeys by individuals or groups to a place of religious importance
relics Physical remains of a holy person's life, which might include the bones or blood of a saint or object that the saint used or touched. In the Middle Ages, people believed relics could work miracles.
Roman Empire The people and lands that belonged to ancient Rome, consisting of most of southern Europe and northern Africa from Britain to the Middle East
saints People identified by the Church as especially holy; ordinary people pray to them, asking for help with particular problems or concerns
scholasticism School of philosophy of the late Middle Ages that tried to use logic to find a rational basis for faith
simony Buying or selling of a position within a church
synagogue Jewish house of worship
theology The study of religious faiths

urther Information

ooks:

tkinson, Kenneth. *Judaism* (Religions of the World). Philadelphia: Chelsea House, 2004.

artlidge, Cherese. *The Crusades: Failed Holy Wars* (History's Great Defeats). San Diego: Lucent Books, 2002.

lark, Charles. *Islam* (Religions of the World). San Diego: Greenhaven Press, 2001.

lallick, Mary P. *The Story of Icons.* Holy Cross Press, 2001.

linds, Kathryn. *The Church* (Life in the Middle Ages). New York: Benchmark Books, 2000.

ace, William W. *The Medieval Cathedral* (Building History Series). San Diego: Lucent, 2001.

Veb Sites:

he Middle Ages
www.learner.org/exhibits/middleages
his web site is created for the Annenberg Foundation and the Corporation for Public Broadcasting. has information on various medieval topics, including religion.

JetSERF (The Internet Connection for Medieval Resources)
www.netserf.org
his web site has many links organized by topic. Check the topics under the headings "Philosophy" nd "Religion" and also "Cathedrals and Churches" (under "Architecture") and "Saints and Martyrs" under "Women").

ideos/DVDs:

hartres Cathedral: A Sacred Geometry. Janson Video, 2002 (DVD).

hristianity: The First Thousand Years and Christianity: The Second Thousand Years. A&E ntertainment, 2001 (VHS, DVD).

slam: Empire of Faith. PBS Home Video, 2001 (VHS, DVD).

he Middle Ages. Goldhil Video, 2001 (VHS).

he Popes: The Legacy of Peter. A&E Entertainment, 2005 (VHS, DVD).

Index

Acre, 27
Agnes, Saint, 13
Aleppo, 26, 27
Alexander V, pope, 37
Alfonso III, king of Portugal, 24
Allah, 40, 41
All Saints' Day, 9
Almohads, 42–43
Ambrose, 8
Anastasius I, emperor, 18
anchorites, 13, 36
Anglicanism, 23
Antioch, Battle of, 26, 27
apostles, 8, 13
Arabic language, 40
Aragon, 24
Arius (Arians), 7, 8
Augustine, 8, 9
Avignon, palace at, 36

baptism, 16
Becket, Thomas, 12, 20–21
Beghards, 34
Beguines, 33–34
bishops, 8, 15, 16, 20, 28, 37, 38
Black Death, 43
Bohemia, 35, 37
Boniface VIII, pope, 22
Burgos Cathedral (Spain), 30
Byzantine Empire, 26–28, 38, 40

Callistus II, pope, 20
canon law, 16
Carcassonne, France, 34, 35
cardinals, 15, 16, 36
Castile, 24
Cathars, 34–35
cathedrals, 4, 6, 12, 14, 23, 28, 36, 42
Catholic Church, *See* Roman Catholic Church
Cerularius, Michael, 9, 38
Charlemagne, 18
Chartres Cathedral (France), 4, 13, 29
Children's Crusade, 27
Christianity, 4
  beginnings of, 6
  defining faith of, 7–8
  differing beliefs in, 38
  expansion and division of, 8–9
  Muslims converting to, 41
church and state, 18–23
churches, 7, 8, 16–17, 32
"Church Fathers," 8
Church offices, appointments to, 20, 22
Church of the Holy Sepulcher (Jerusalem), 11
Church organization, 8
Clare of Assisi, 33
Clement V, pope, 36
Clement VII, pope, 37
clergy, 8, 13, 15, 16
confession, 16
Constance, Council of, 37
Constantine, emperor, 7, 8, 18, 20
Constantinople, 8, 9, 26–28, 38, 39, 40
councils, Christian, 8, 13, 16, 18, 20, 35, 37, 38
Crusader States, 26
Crusades, 5, 26–28, 43
Cyril, 40

Damascus, 26
Day of Judgment, 11
deacons, 16
Demetrius, Saint, 38
Díaz de Vivar, Rodrigo (El Cid), 24
divorce, 22
doctrine, 31
Dominican order, 35
Donation of Constantine, 20
Dorylaeum, Battle of, 26, 27

Eastern Orthodox Church, 5, 9, 38–40
Eckhart, Meister, 35
Edessa, 26
education, *See* schools; universities
excommunication, 9, 13, 20, 38

Ferdinand, king, 24, 25
festivals, 9, 13
Five Pillars of Islam, 41
Fourth Lateran Council, 16
Franciscan order, 32, 33, 34
Francis of Assisi, 32, 33
friars, 32, 33, 35

Germanic peoples, 5, 10
Gospels, 7, 40
Gothic style, 28–30
government, 5, 18–22
Granada, king of, 24–25
Great Schism, 37
Gregory IV, pope, 9
Gregory VII, pope, 15, 18–20, 22
Gregory XI, pope, 36
Guiscard, Robert, 22
Guzman, Domingo de, 35

Hagia Sophia (Turkey), 38–40
Hattin, Battle of, 26, 27
Henry II, king of England, 20–21
Henry IV, king of Germany, 18–20, 22
Henry V, king of Germany, 20
heresy, 8, 34–35, 36
hermits, 13, 14
Hildegard of Bingen, 36
holidays (holy days), 5, 9
Holy Land, 12, 26, 43
Holy Roman Empire, 20, 35
Hus, John, 35, 37

indulgences, 23
Innocent III, pope, 20, 32, 35
Inquisition, 35, 36
Isabella, Queen, 24, 25
Islam, 4, 10, 31, 40–42. *See also* Muslim(s)

James, Saint, 12, 13
Jerome, 8
Jerusalem, 12, 26, 27
Jesus, 6, 7, 11, 12, 13, 32, 39, 41
Jews, 24, 38, 41–43
John, king of England, 20
John XXII, pope, 37
Judaism, 5, 6. *See also* Jews
Julian of Norwich, 36
Justinian, Emperor, 40

last rites, 16
law(s), 5
  against Jews, 43
  canon, 16
  Muslim, 40–41
lay investiture, 18–20
Leo III, pope, 18
Leo IX, pope, 9, 14–15, 38
León (Spain), 24
Louis VII, king of France, 26

Magyars, 10
marriage, 15, 16
Martin V, pope, 37
martyrs, 13
Mary, 13, 14
Methodius, 40
miracles, 13
monasteries, 8, 10, 13, 14, 23, 26, 28, 31, 36
monks, 8, 10, 14, 15, 28
Moses Maimonides, 42
mosque of Córdoba (Spain), 42
Muhammad, 40, 41
Muslim(s): 5
  Crusades, 26–28
  invasions by, 10
  meaning of term, 40
  Reconquista, 24–26
mystics, 32, 35–36

Navarre, 24
Nicaea, Council of, 8, 9, 18
Nicholas, Saint, 13
Nicholas II, pope, 15, 22
Normans, 22, 26
Novgorod Cathedral, 40

pagans, 8–9, 38
papacy:
  authority of, 9
  clash between rulers and, 18–20
  electing the pope, 15
  multiple popes, 36–37
  origin of, 8
  politics of, 21–22, 37
  power of, 15, 16
Papal States, 21–22
parishioners, 16
parliaments, 5
Passover, 43
patriarchs, 38
Patrick, Saint, 13
patron saints, 13
Paul, 6, 12, 13
peace movement, 13–14
penance, 16, 20, 23
Pepin the Short, 18, 21
Peter, 8, 12
Peter IV, king, 43
Philip IV, king of France, 22
pilgrimages, 12–13, 41
Poor Clares, 33
popes, *See* papacy
Porete, Marguerite, 35–36
Portugal, 24
priests, 6, 8, 15, 16
Protestantism, 23
Protestant Reformation, 23, 4
purgatory, 23

Ravenna Church (Italy), 7
Reconquista, 24–26
reform, 14, 15
relics, 13, 23
Roman Catholic Church, 5, 6, 10–37
  attacks on heretics, 34–35
  badges for Jews required by, 43
  celebration of Mass, 5
  challenges to, 32–37
  clashes between popes and rulers, 18–20
  and Crusades, 26–28
  intellectual activity in, 28, 3
  mystics, 35–36
  origin of, 9
  reform in, 14, 15
  rise of religious feeling, 11–13, 28
  split with Eastern Orthodox Church, 9, 38
Roman Empire, 4, 6, 7, 8, 18
Rome, bishop of, 8

saints, 9, 12, 13, 20, 28, 33
Saladin, 26
Santiago de Compostela (Spain), 12, 13
scholarship, 24, 26, 28, 31
scholasticism, 31
schools, 4–5, 28, 31, 41
Sigismund, Holy Roman Emperor, 35, 37
simony, 15
Slavs, conversion of, 40
stained glass, 29
Stephen II, pope, 18
synagogues, 43

Theodosius, emperor, 7
theology, 28, 31, 35, 36
Thomas Aquinas, Saint, 31
Truce of God, 13

universities, 4–5, 28, 31
Urban II, pope, 26
Urban VI, pope, 36–37

Vikings, 10
Vladimir, Prince, 39, 40

Waldensians, 33, 34
Waldo, Peter, 32–33
Wycliffe, John, 35

Zaragoza, king of, 24